Purchased with
Monies Donated
In Memory
Of
Roy Naismith

MONSTERS

WEREWOLVES

BY TONEY ALLMAN

KIDHAVEN PRESS

An imprint of Thomson Gale, a part of The Thomson Corporation

Detroit • New York • San Francisco • San Diego • New Haven, Conn.
Waterville, Maine • London • Munich

Picture Credits

Cover: © C.Walker/Topham/The Image Works
© Avco Embassy/The Kobal Collection, 5
© Bridgeman Art Library, 39
© Oscar Burriel/Photo Researchers, Inc., 30
CDC, 25 (bottom), 26 (both)
© Fortean Picture Library, 9, 10
© Kismet Entertainment Group/The Kobal Collection, 6
© Mary Evans Picture Library, 14, 17
© Dr. F. A. Murphy/Visuals Unlimited, 25 (inset)
© Photofest, 33, 34, 36
© Leonard de Selva/CORBIS, 23, 29
© Charles Walker/Topham/The Image Works, 16, 19, 21

© 2005 Thomson Gale, a part of The Thomson Corporation.

Thomson and Star Logo are trademarks and Gale and KidHaven Press are registered trademarks used herein under license.

For more information, contact
KidHaven Press
27500 Drake Rd.
Farmington Hills, MI 48331-3535
Or you can visit our Internet site at http://www.gale.com

LIBRARY OF CONGRESS CATALOGING-IN-PUBLICATION DATA

Allman, Toney.
  Werewolves / by Toney Allman.
    p. cm. — (Monsters)
  Includes bibliographical references and index.
  ISBN 0-7377-2620-2 (hardcover : alk. paper)
  1. Werewolves. I. Title. II. Monsters series (KidHaven Press)
  GR830.W4A57 2005
  398'.469–dc22

                                                    2004013489

Printed in the United States of America

CONTENTS

Chapter 1

Werewolves Among Us

Werewolves are people who can change into wolves. A werewolf is a person who might look as normal as anyone, but in the dark of night, a **transformation** takes place. The normal-seeming person becomes a bloodthirsty beast that threatens any living creature that crosses its path. Some people say the werewolf changes his or her form into a real wolf. Other stories say that the werewolf keeps the shape of a human body but has the head of a wolf. Some tales describe a human who grows fur, claws, and fangs. However it looks, the werewolf is a killer, fearsome and cruel.

For hundreds of years, **folklore** has told of these terrifying monsters. The people who told these legends

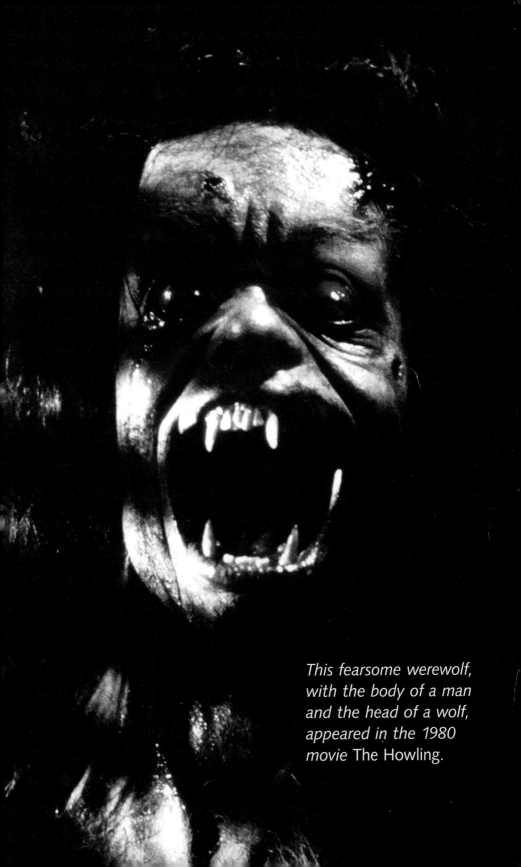

This fearsome werewolf, with the body of a man and the head of a wolf, appeared in the 1980 movie The Howling.

lived in Europe during medieval times, from about the fifth century to the sixteenth century. They lived during a time when real wolf packs roamed the countryside. These people were not very educated. **Superstition**, not science, guided their lives. There were superstitious legends for everything. People learned old folktales and superstitions to explain things they did not understand. They believed in magic, sorcerers, witches, demons that walked the earth, and werewolves. Werewolf legends grew and grew until everyone believed that werewolves were a dreadful, magical danger that no one wanted to encounter.

The Ways of the Werewolf

All folklore taught a few ways to tell if a person might be a werewolf. In human form, the werewolf has

A werewolf from the 2002 movie Dog Soldiers *hunts for victims under the cover of darkness.*

bushy eyebrows that meet in a point in the middle of the forehead. The teeth may be slightly red or black. Fingernails are long, and hair grows on the palms of the hands. The second and third fingers are the same length. The skin is pale. The person's eyes and mouth are dry, and he or she is always thirsty. The body is usually covered with cuts and scratches, received from running through brush and thorns while in wolf form.

Werewolves are creatures of darkness. As wolves, they hunt at night, with eyes gleaming green or red. They search for raw meat and fresh blood. Werewolves in wolf form mutilate flocks of sheep and herds of cattle. They kill and eat people, especially tasty children.

When morning comes, the werewolf changes back to his or her human body. Sometimes, werewolves are happy with the murderous lives they are leading. Sometimes, however, werewolves wish they could be normal and are sorry for their crimes. Not every werewolf chose to be a werewolf.

BECOMING A WEREWOLF

Many pathways lead to werewolfery. In medieval eastern Europe, people believed in powerful sorcerers who could control the spirit world and forces of nature. These sorcerers could transform themselves into wolves whenever they wished. They could also curse their enemies and make them werewolves against their will.

People forced to become werewolves were often sad and tried not to do too much harm. They usually did not attack people and only stole a cow or sheep if they were starving. One very old story describes the misery of becoming a werewolf because of a curse. It tells about a young farmer who was loved by a witch. The young man did not return the witch's love so she cursed him:

> One day, grazing his cattle in the woods, he decided he would cut some wood. As he raised his axe, however, he saw his hands becoming paws before his very eyes. He looked on helplessly while his fingernails turned into curling claws, and great tufts of hair started to sprout all over his body. When he ran to his cows, intending to herd them quickly home, they stampeded in abject terror. He sought to call them back, but could only howl. To his horror, he realized he was now a wild and lonely werewolf.[1]

Other werewolves were not so unhappy. They chose to become werewolves because they were evil. These people became werewolves by making deals with the devil. In return for selling their souls, they learned magic that turned them into werewolves.

A Dark Werewolf Ritual

An ancient **ritual** for becoming a werewolf was written down long ago: At night, the man who wished to become a werewolf found a flat place on a mountaintop and drew a circle in the dirt. There, he built a fire,

over which he hung an iron pot full of water. Into the pot went several magic plants, such as poppy seeds, opium, hemlock, and nightshade. As the steam rose from the pot, the man would chant his evil spell:

> Hail, hail, hail, great Wolf Spirit, hail!
> A **boon** I ask thee, mighty **shade**,
> Within this circle I have made.
> Make me a werewolf strong and bold,
> The terror alike of young and old.[2]

A hungry werewolf pounces on a helpless woman in this illustration.

Next, the man had to strip himself naked, rub his body with a magic **salve**, and wrap a wolf skin around his waist. He breathed in the steam from his pot and felt the salve tingle on his skin. Then he would feel his body begin to change. His nails began to grow into claws. His skin felt the prickliness of new fur. Ready to serve the powers of evil, he shouted into the night sky:

Make me a man-eater.
Make me a woman-eater.
Make me a child-eater.
Make me a werewolf![3]

In this sixteenth-century woodcut, a werewolf attacks a villager outside his home.

Some werewolves, old stories say, learned this ritual from the devil or his demons. A demon would give the salve and wolf skin to the person in return for his soul. Other people were said to have learned their powers from other werewolves.

Werewolves by Fate

Some people did not need rituals to become werewolves. A boy born at midnight on Christmas Eve was said to be condemned to be a werewolf. Each Christmas season for the rest of his life, he would turn into a wolf. No matter how gentle he was as a human, he killed in his wolf form. His only escape was his own death.

People could also become werewolves by accident. For example, a person who was bitten by a werewolf would become a werewolf. In some tales, people who drank the water from certain streams where real wolves drank would become werewolves. Just drinking the water from a wolf's footprint could turn a person into a werewolf. No matter how the werewolf was created, he or she lived a dark life of cruelty and killing.

Defense Against Werewolves

When a werewolf attacked, survival was not easy. The werewolf was bigger, stronger, faster, and smarter than real wolves. Sometimes, a werewolf could be frightened away from its victim with the threat of bright torches and bullets from rescuers. Old stories and folklore told of only a few other ways to fight the werewolf.

The best way to stop a werewolf was to catch it and make three cuts in its forehead. If the werewolf saw the blood dripping from the cuts, transformation stopped, and the evil one was a werewolf no longer. The trouble was that catching a werewolf without being killed oneself was almost impossible.

A person being attacked by a werewolf could try running into a field of rye. Werewolves hated rye grain and could not follow. A werewolf could also be trapped in wolf shape if a brave person stole its clothes. Without clothes, the werewolf could not change back to human form and was condemned forever to run as a wolf.

Is It True?

Belief in werewolves was once very strong. During medieval times, people were sure that werewolves were real. They heard many stories of werewolf killings and lived in terror of werewolf crimes.

CHAPTER 2

WEREWOLF TALES

Many stories from many different times and places were told about werewolves. By the 1500s, people were certain that werewolves roamed everywhere, day and night. People were hysterically frightened of the werewolves they thought lived among them. Thousands of people were accused of being werewolves, captured, tried in courts, convicted, and often executed.

THE WEREWOLF PEETER STUBBE

One famous werewolf case was reported in 1591. The story was published in a small booklet called a tract and was signed by several witnesses who swore it was true. Throughout Europe, people read in this tract

A group of peasants stops a werewolf from devouring a child in this eighteenth-century painting.

about the terrible werewolf named Peeter Stubbe. Stubbe lived in a small town in Germany, where many unsolved murders took place over a period of twenty-five years. The mutilated bodies of men, women, and children were found by horrified towns-

people. It seemed obvious to them that a vicious beast was on the loose.

One of the very few people to meet this werewolf and survive was a little girl. Along with some other children, she was playing in a pasture one day beside a herd of cows and newborn calves. The tract explains, "And suddenly among these children comes this vile wolf running and caught the pretty fine girl by the collar, with intent to pull out her throat."[4] Luckily, the child was wearing a coat with a tight, stiff collar that protected her neck. Her frightened playmates ran away, but the cows, afraid for the calves, stampeded toward the wolf and scared him off with their horns. The wolf ran away, and so the little girl was saved.

A Werewolf Revealed

Other victims were not so lucky. More deaths occurred. Some people just disappeared. Finally a group of hunters with dogs entered the nearby forest, determined to find the werewolf. The dogs took off, chasing a wolf. The hunters hurried to catch up. They knew the wolf was surrounded by their dogs and could not escape. When they caught up with the dogs, the hunters were shocked to discover that the wolf had vanished, and in his place stood a villager, Peeter Stubbe. The only explanation they could think of was that Stubbe was a werewolf. One hunter swore he saw Stubbe change from wolf to man before his eyes. The men grabbed Stubbe and arrested him.

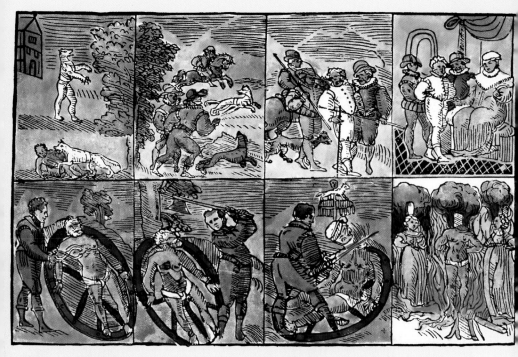

This sixteenth-century woodcut shows the execution of Peeter Stubbe, who confessed to being a werewolf.

At his trial, Stubbe was threatened with torture if he did not confess. He admitted he was a werewolf. He said the devil had given him a wolf skin. According to the tract, he put the wolf skin on and became "a greedy, devouring wolf, strong and mighty, with eyes great and large, which in the night sparkled like unto brands of fire, a mouth great and wide, with most sharp and cruel teeth, a huge body and mighty paws."[5] Stubbe even told the court where he had hidden his wolf skin. The townspeople went to search for the wolf skin, but they could not find it. They figured the devil had come and taken it back. Stubbe confessed that he killed and ate many people in his wolf form. He was convicted of werewolfery and executed for his crimes.

THE TEENAGED WEREWOLF

Stubbe was only one of many people who confessed that they were werewolves. In 1603, a teenaged boy in France, Jean Grenier, claimed to be a werewolf. Terrible things were happening in the countryside where Grenier lived. Children disappeared from roads and fields, but their bodies were never found. The people believed that a werewolf was roaming among them.

French villagers hunt a werewolf in this nineteenth-century illustration from a storybook.

One day, thirteen-year-old Marguerite Poirer was guarding sheep in a pasture when a wolf attacked her. She hit the wolf with her shepherd's staff and successfully drove it away. Later in the day, Grenier told her he had been the wolf. He said he would have eaten her if she had not hit him with the stick. Grenier was a dirty, wild, strange-looking boy. Frightened, Marguerite reported his words in the village. Her story was backed up by another girl, eighteen-year-old Jeanne Gaboriaut, who reported that Grenier told her he sometimes wore a wolf skin. He had said to her: "I have killed dogs and drunk their blood, but little girls taste better . . . I am a werewolf!"[6]

Grenier was arrested and quickly admitted to the court that he was a werewolf. He claimed to have eaten several children. He explained that one night in the forest, he had met the devil, a dark man on a black horse. The devil had given Grenier a wolf skin and a magic salve to turn him into a cruel wolf. Many people believed Grenier's story, but he was not executed. The judge thought the boy was mentally ill and his story of transformation untrue. Grenier was committed for life to a monastery, where religious men could look after him. Grenier lived there for eight years before he died, a pitiful, crazy-acting person.

The Werewolf of Gevaudan

As the years passed, most people of Europe lost their fear of werewolves. By the 1700s, people were no longer being tried and executed for sorcery, witchcraft, or werewolfery. Still, belief in werewolves had not died.

The monstrous Werewolf of Gevaudan holds a female victim in his powerful jaws in this eighteenth-century illustration.

Between 1764 and 1767, villagers reported a werewolf roaming a rural mountain area of France.

The first sighting of the werewolf came in 1764. A woman herding cows reported seeing a huge wolf, as big as a cow or donkey. Luckily, her cattle chased it away with their horns. A month later, a little girl was killed by a wolf. As time went by, more villagers were attacked and killed by some beast. People were terrified. Many hunters went out to kill the beast, but they always failed. Several times, the beast was wounded, left a trail of blood as it escaped, and even fell down only to rise again. As the wolf attacked over and over, people became certain it was no ordinary animal. The giant wolf must be a loup-garou, the French word for werewolf.

HUNTING DOWN THE KILLER

In 1765, the French king sent his troops to kill the beast. More than one hundred wolves were killed. One soldier did kill a giant wolf. Most people in the village celebrated, thinking the werewolf was dead. One woman, however, was not so sure. She said: "I know it is still alive, out there, watching us from the shadows! It will get me, I just know it!"[7] She was right. After the king's troops went home, the killings continued. Nobody knew if the werewolf could ever be stopped.

Finally, in 1767, three hundred men organized in a hunt to find and kill the beast. One of them, Jean Chastel, had silver bullets blessed by a priest. He sat in his hunting spot with an open prayer book, waiting for the other hunters to chase the beast toward him.

Hunters try to kill the Werewolf of Gevaudan as the beast attacks a baby.

When a wolf appeared, Chastel shot twice, and the wolf fell dead. This time, it was the right beast. When the hunters cut open its belly, they found human bones inside. The wolf truly was a huge creature. It was so big that its body was displayed not only in the village but all around France. Some people believed that the beast was just an unusually large wolf, but many were sure that it was a werewolf that had finally been caught. They could not imagine a normal wolf could be so big, so smart, or so hard to kill.

Explaining strange events can be hard when people have little scientific knowledge about the world or nature. Weird things are called magic, witchcraft, and deals with the devil. Murders, wolf attacks, and even odd people were linked together in tales that kept the idea of werewolves alive.

Chapter 3

How to Explain Werewolves

Superstition and ignorance can explain some werewolf stories, but scientists and researchers also try to understand how the folklore grew. Today they wonder why people were so sure that they saw werewolves or so willing to admit to being werewolves. Scientists want to know what people saw and experienced that made the legends begin. Modern medicine might have some of the answers.

A Disease That Makes Fur

A couple of unusual diseases could have seemed to ignorant medieval people to prove that werewolves existed. One such disease is called **hypertrichosis**. People with this disease are born with long hair covering their bodies. The disease is extremely rare. Only fifty cases have been reported in the last five hundred years. However, paintings from hundreds of years ago show people who had this disease. One family with hypertrichosis lived with the king of France in the 1500s. He liked them so much that he gave them a rich life in his palace. However, medieval villagers might not have accepted these people. People with very long body hair may have been seen as wolflike creatures.

PORPHYRIA

Another disease that scientists have linked to werewolf ideas is called **porphyria**. It is a rare disease, but many symptoms of the disease match descriptions of werewolves. Today, people born with porphyria can

This seventeenth-century drawing shows a man with werewolf characteristics. Victims of the rare disease hypertrichosis may have been mistaken for werewolves in the middle ages.

be treated, but in its most severe form, it caused much suffering in medieval times. Porphyria victims have very sensitive eyes and skin. Sunshine hurts them and causes rashes to appear. These people are comfortable going outside only at night. They are pale or yellowish. Shaving hurts too much, so men with porphyria often let their beards grow. Sores form on porphyria victims' bodies. Sometimes skin sores grow so big that faces are mutilated and fingers become like claws. Teeth turn slightly red or brown. People suffering with porphyria can also behave strangely. They may act wildly and yell and howl.

Ignorant people are often fearful of anyone who is different. Someone with an illness that is rare and hard to understand could be seen as evil or cursed. Many porphyria symptoms match what people think of as werewolf behavior. The cuts and scratches on werewolves from running through thorns could have been the sores and rashes of porphyria. Sick people who disliked daylight could have seemed strange or evil. Howling could have seemed animal-like. Perhaps porphyria victims were thought to be werewolves by their neighbors.

RABIES

Scientists also wonder if werewolf folklore arose from **rabies** symptoms. Rabies is a terrifying disease that is passed from animals to people through **saliva** and bites. The victims always die, but not before they act absolutely crazy. A rabid wolf is vicious. It attacks and

bites anyone or anything that comes near. It is not at all like a regular wolf. History provides much evidence of rabies epidemics, among people and animals, during medieval times. Rabid wolves were a terrible danger in villages and farmlands.

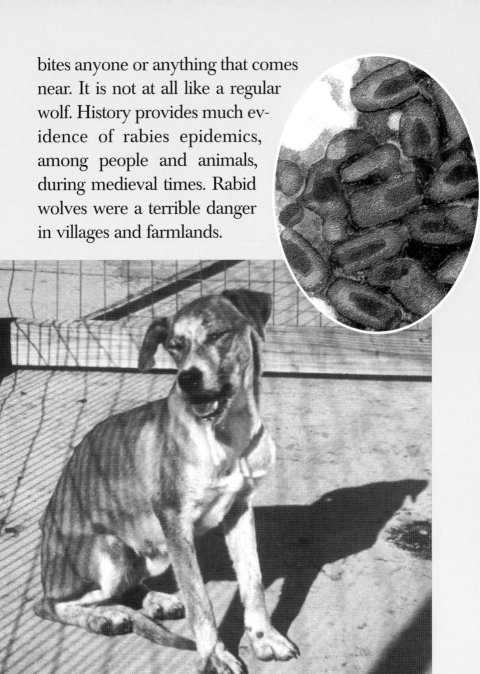

The rabies virus, shown above magnified (inset), is passed from animals to people through saliva and bites. Pictured is a rabid dog.

If a person is bitten by a rabid wolf, he or she will get rabies, too. Drinking from streams or out of a wolf's footprint could give a person rabies if wolf saliva were in the water. In a way, contact with wolves changes normal people into something else. Today, shots can prevent rabies from developing, but this was not possible in medieval times.

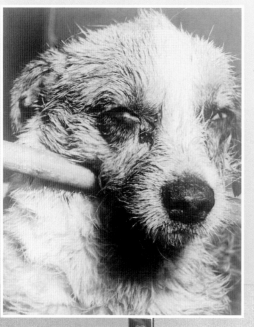

This man became infected with rabies after a rabid dog (left) bit him.

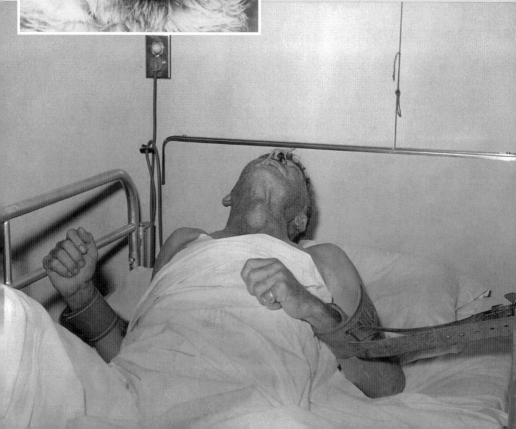

People with rabies are out of their heads, unable to control themselves. They act wildly and violently. They have fits of rage, scratching and biting people who care for them. Sometimes, rabies victims are so strong and violent that five people cannot hold them still. Victims may scream and even make coughing, barking sounds. Rabies victims are terribly thirsty but cannot drink any water. They foam at the mouth, just like vicious animals.

Many rabies symptoms sound like werewolf behavior. Werewolves are supposed to be superstrong and vicious. Werewolves are always thirsty, too. Hundreds of years ago, people had never heard of germs. They did not know how diseases were passed from person to person or from animals to people. Perhaps a sick, violent, rabid wolf was believed to be a magic wolf—a werewolf. Perhaps people crazed with rabies acted so much like animals that the behavior seemed wolflike. Rabies epidemics could explain some werewolf legends.

MIND-ALTERING DRUGS

Still, many people claimed to be werewolves even though they were not suffering from diseases. Some of these people were probably murderers who confessed to werewolf crimes to avoid torture. Some people, however, actually believed they were werewolves. Many researchers think drugs could have caused these people to believe they were werewolves.

The old recipes for magic salves and ritual brews included plants that were powerful poisons and mind-altering drugs. These drugs could be breathed into the lungs or absorbed through the skin. They could cause a person to have strong visions or dreams that seemed real. Such experiences are called **hallucinations**. People who have hallucinations see or experience things that are not actually happening. If a person believed that he or she could transform into a wolf, such powerful drugs could make the person hallucinate that it was so. When the person awoke, he or she could truly believe that wolf experiences had occurred.

POISON IN THE GRAIN

Hallucinations also can happen to people who do not take drugs on purpose. In the past, most villages grew rye and made it into bread. A poisonous fungus called **ergot** sometimes grows on rye. People who eat bread contaminated with ergot have hallucinations, experience terrible confusion, and act crazy. Ergot poisoning could have been common in medieval times.

In 1951, doctors in France saw an example of ergot poisoning for themselves. One hundred thirty-five people turned up at a hospital after eating rye bread contaminated with ergot. A few of these people were so poisoned that they died. Others had horrible hallucinations that they were being attacked by tigers and snakes. Some became so crazy that they thought they were wild animals. Doctors were able to cure these people with modern medicine, but medieval people

Some scientists believe that werewolves were only hallucinations, like those shown in this eighteenth-century illustration.

had no such medicines. After seeing the French people with ergot poisoning, researchers wondered if ergot hallucinations affected medieval villages. Poisoned villagers may have become so ill and confused that they thought they were or saw werewolves.

THE WOLF SICKNESS

Drugs and poisons can make people see things that are not there, but so can mental illnesses. People with mental illnesses no longer know what is real. Rarely, people can develop mental illnesses that make them

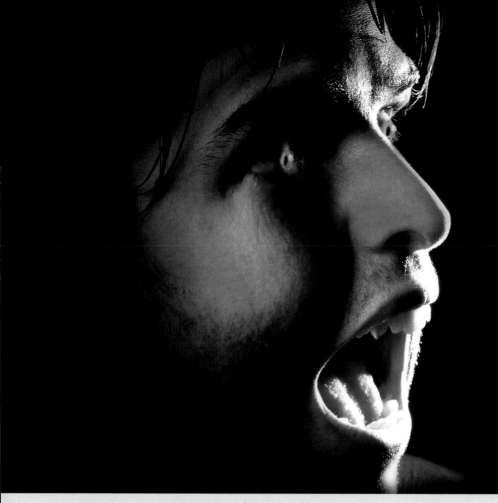

Sufferers of the mental illness lycanthropy like this man truly believe they are werewolves.

believe they are werewolves. **Lycanthropy** is the name of this mental illness. A person with lycanthropy insists that he or she is a werewolf. Lycanthropy could be why some people in medieval times claimed they were werewolves.

In the 1970s, one forty-nine-year-old American woman was mentally ill with lycanthropy. She was so

sure she was a wolf that she looked in the mirror and saw a wolf face, even when doctors told her that her face had not changed. She stripped off her clothes and crawled around on all fours. She gnawed on the furniture and grunted and growled. She said to her doctors: "I am a wolf of the night: I am a wolf woman of the day . . . I have claws, teeth, fangs, hair."[8] This woman was hospitalized and cured with modern medicine, but no medicines for lycanthropy existed hundreds of years ago. Mental illnesses were usually believed to be caused by the devil or a curse.

Of course, lycanthropy is a very unusual mental illness. No matter what explanations scientists use for werewolfery, no one knows for sure why so many reports of werewolves were made in history. Most educated people today think of werewolves as just superstition, but the scary legends about real werewolves have not been forgotten.

CHAPTER 4

FUN WITH WEREWOLVES

Werewolf sightings may be rare today, but scary werewolves live on in movies, books, games, music, and even sports. New werewolf stories have been told, and werewolf lore has changed. Nowadays, werewolves can once again be good people sadly cursed, just as in ancient times. Sometimes they are even cute or funny.

WEREWOLVES IN MOVIES

The modern American werewolf was born in 1941, in a movie called *The Wolf Man* produced by Universal Pictures. The werewolf in this movie was played by Lon Chaney Jr., and he scared so many people with his monster that the movie was a popular hit. Chaney

The Wolf Man, played by actor Lon Chaney Jr., stalks a young woman in the 1941 film The Wolf Man.

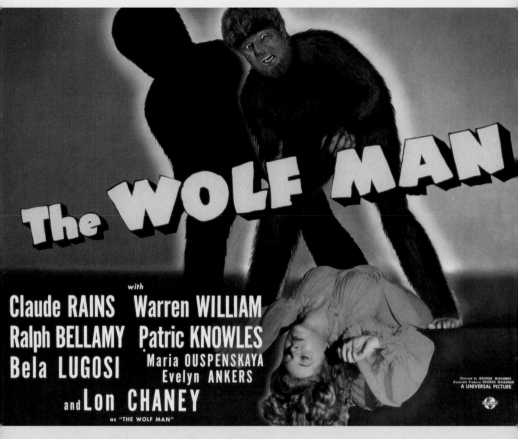

with
Claude RAINS   Warren WILLIAM
Ralph BELLAMY   Patric KNOWLES
Bela LUGOSI   Maria OUSPENSKAYA
Evelyn ANKERS
and Lon CHANEY
as "THE WOLF MAN"

Directed by GEORGE WAGGNER
Associate Producer GEORGE WAGGNER
A UNIVERSAL PICTURE

The Wolf Man *was a popular hit, and the first of many Hollywood werewolf movies.*

played a young man named Larry Talbot. The normally gentle Talbot became a werewolf when he was bitten in a fight with a wolf that was attacking a woman.

In the movie, the wolf that bit Talbot was a werewolf. The bite disappeared magically, and in its place was a star mark called a pentagram that marks all werewolves and their victims. Talbot became a werewolf against his will, but he did not look like a real wolf. He was a monster in human form with fur, fangs,

claws, and an evil mind. At night, he hunted and killed human victims. By day, he was horrified by the crimes he committed as a werewolf, but he could not stop himself. In the end, as Talbot the werewolf attacked a young woman, he was beaten to death by his father with a silver-headed cane. As the werewolf lay dying, it turned back into the shape of Talbot before his father's grief-stricken eyes.

The public loved Chaney's portrayal of the doomed Talbot and the evil werewolf he became. Chaney made a convincing werewolf, even though monster makeup was not very good in 1941. Chaney transformed into a werewolf with just some yak hair, spirit gum, and cotton. Still, that werewolf was very real to moviegoers. Werewolf movies today continue to show werewolves as human monsters, like *The Wolf Man,* instead of as people who change into wolves.

The Wolf Man was only the beginning for werewolf movies. Lon Chaney Jr. played a werewolf brought back from the grave in several more monster movies. As time passed, other actors brought werewolves to life again and again in scary, sometimes violent monster movies.

Werewolves of Song

The song and music used in one movie even became a hit song called "Werewolves of London," which was written and sung by Warren Zevon. The werewolf in this song howls and kills, but he is also funny. He gets a drink in a bar, eats Chinese food, and even visits with the queen. People who like creepy rock music can also enjoy listening to the Young Werewolves. This rock band from Philadelphia, Pennsylvania, loves to howl as part of its act.

WEREWOLVES ON TV

Even television got into the werewolf act, but werewolves on TV could be funny. Between 1964 and 1966, a comedy show called *The Munsters* featured a little boy werewolf. Edward Wolfgang Munster lived in a normal American town with his not-so-normal American family. They were all monsters! Eddie's father was Frankenstein's monster. His mother was a vampire

Eddie Munster and his werewolf doll Woof Woof starred in the 1960s television comedy show The Munsters.

whose last name was Dracula before she got married. Eddie himself acted like a regular little boy who went to school and ran in track races. But he was not quite like other boys. He had pointed ears and green skin. Eddie also had a favorite werewolf doll named Woof Woof. He and his parents hoped Eddie would grow into a strong, healthy, teenage werewolf. People laughed at werewolf Eddie and his monster family, but Eddie did not frighten anyone who watched the show.

WEREWOLF FUN AND GAMES

Today, even when people play werewolf games, they like to be a little bit frightened. Party games and role-playing games with very ugly werewolves are available for people who want to enjoy werewolf legends. One party game, The Werewolves of Miller's Hollow, pits werewolves against villagers in a contest to see who can identify the werewolf first—without being eaten! To win, the villagers have to figure out who is the werewolf. Werewolves win if they can hide their identities from the other players.

More complicated are the role-playing fantasy games such as the White Wolf Game Studio game called Werewolf: The Apocalypse. Players in this fantasy game pretend they are an ancient group of **shape-shifters**. All the players divide into different tribes, make up rules for getting along with each other, and fight evil vampires in order to survive. In this game, werewolves are not evil; they are misunderstood beings from a fantasy world.

Werewolves in Books

No monster or fantasy game would be complete without werewolves, and the same is true for scary books. The Goosebumps series for kids by R.L. Stine includes werewolf tales. One of the books, *Werewolf Skin*, tells the adventures of twelve-year-old Alex Hunter. He visits the town of Wolf Creek to stay with his aunt and uncle and soon discovers that it is not an ordinary place. On Halloween night, under a full moon, Alex faces terrible danger from a pair of real werewolves. He watches two people use wolf-skin capes to magically transform into wolves. Just as in medieval times, there are many modern ways to become a werewolf.

In J.K. Rowling's Harry Potter series, the werewolf is a teacher at Harry's school. Professor Lupin became a werewolf as a child when he was bitten by a werewolf. He is a good, kindhearted man who only becomes a werewolf during the full moon. Magic potions can control his transformations, but much as Lupin wishes it, there is no cure for his werewolfery. Lupin is a werewolf true to the ancient folklore. Unlike movie monsters in human shapes, he roams at night in real wolf form.

Sports

People who admire the strength and cunning of werewolves sometimes give themselves werewolf nicknames. One ice hockey team for kids with special needs in New York is named Werewolves of London.

A werewolf attacks a girl on the cover of a French storybook called *The Werewolf*.

The young Werewolves skate, play hockey, and compete with other teams in their league. With practice, the players try to become fast, smart, strong, and maybe even a little scary—just like the werewolves of old. A minor league baseball team in Canada lived up to their Werewolves name. In 1999, they won the Frontier League Championship.

WEREWOLVES EVERYWHERE

Of course, the best time for werewolves in modern life is Halloween. On that holiday, werewolf hands, masks, and costumes are sold to millions of people who want to transform into werewolves for at least one night. People can also buy werewolf decorations to hang in dark rooms or on porches and frighten Halloween visitors.

Werewolves can be found at haunted houses and in graveyards on dark, creepy Halloween nights throughout America. At Thrillvania Theme Park in Texas, visitors can enter Verdun Manor and test their courage as they face down the horrible werewolves that haunt the mansion. The werewolf costumes are carefully made and very elaborate. Actors wear wolf heads and realistic fur, and they have snarls of rage and gleaming werewolf eyes. The werewolves prowl Verdun Manor, looking for unsuspecting victims to eat. On Halloween, werewolves roam the earth once again, just as they did in medieval times. Beware to all careless people who intrude where the werewolves walk.

NOTES

Chapter 1: Werewolves Among Us

1. Charles Phillips and Michael Kerrigan, *Forests of the Vampire: Slavic Myth.* New York: Barnes and Noble, 1999, p. 123.

2. Quoted in Editors of Time-Life Books, *Transformations.* Alexandria, VA: Time-Life, 1989, p. 95.

3. Quoted in Editors of Time-Life Books, *Transformations,* p. 100.

Chapter 2: Werewolf Tales

4. Quoted in David Harley, "The Trial and Execution of Peeter Stubbe," Witchcraft and the Occult: Werewolves, www.nd.edu/~dharley/witchcraft/texts/Stubbe-Peter.html.

5. Quoted in Harley, "The Trial and Execution of Peeter Stubbe."

6. Quoted in Sabine Baring-Gould, *The Book of Werewolves,* www.horrormasters.com/Text/a0503.pdf.

7. Quoted in Occultopedia, "Gevaudan, Beast of," www.occultopedia.com/g/gevaudan.htm.

Chapter 3: How to Explain Werewolves

8. Quoted in Angela Cybulski, ed., *Fact or Fiction? Werewolves*. San Diego, CA: Greenhaven, 2004, p. 124.

GLOSSARY

boon: A blessing or gift.

ergot: A black fungus that infects some cereal plants, such as rye.

folklore: The traditional beliefs, tales, and practices of a group of people. Often the ideas are false or without a basis in fact.

hallucination: An experience that feels very real but is not actually happening. Usually hallucinations result from mental illnesses or drugs.

hypertrichosis: An inherited disorder in which people are born with long hair covering their bodies.

lycanthropy: A mental disorder in which a person believes he or she is a wolf or other animal.

porphyria: A rare, inherited disease that affects skin, eyes, and sometimes the brain.

rabies: An infectious, viral disease in warm-blooded animals and people. It is transmitted by bites or infected saliva and is fatal.

ritual: A ceremony of religion or worship.

saliva: The watery mixture in the mouth; spit.

salve: An ointment or cream.

shade: A spirit or ghost.

shape-shifter: An imaginary being who can transform from one body shape into another form, such as a sorcerer into a wolf.

superstition: An unreasonable belief that is not logical. Something believed because of ignorance or faith in magic.

transformation: In magical beliefs, the complete change of a body into another body, as from human to wolf.

FOR FURTHER EXPLORATION

BOOKS

Laura Buller and Philip Wilkinson, *Myths and Monsters: From Dragons to Werewolves*. New York: Dorling Kindersley, 2003. Read about all sorts of monsters, witches, werewolves, and dragons.

Sarah Howarth, *Medieval Places*. Brookfield, CT: Millbrook, 1991. Learn about the way people lived during medieval times. Most were peasants who lived in poverty and ignorance.

Ian Thorne, *The Wolf Man*. Mankato, MN: Crestwood House, 1977. This is an old book, but it tells two wonderful werewolf movie stories, complete with black-and-white movie stills and posters. Read "The Wolf Man" and "The Werewolf of London" and learn about other werewolf movies, too.

WEB SITES

Gander Academy's Werewolves (www.stemnet.nf. ca/CITE/monsters_werewolves.htm). This fifth-grade class project contains everything anyone would want to know about werewolves. Read werewolf stories and werewolf history. Discover the important rules for the care and feeding of your own werewolf.

Ghostly, Ghastly, Creepy, Crawly (www. chirpingbird.com/netpets/html/features/oct/ ghostly1.html). Listen to creepy music as you learn about all the ghastly creatures described on this site. There are werewolves, vampires, the Loch Ness monster, Chupacabra, and many more scary things.

Halloween Costumes: Kids' Turn Central (www.kidsturncentral.com/holidays/costumes/hco st1gg.htm). This site features neat ideas for making your own werewolf costume for Halloween.

How We Make Werewolves (http://xoomer. virgilio.it/rseghier/LRP/Trucco/werewolf/ww_suit. html). At this site, experts explain how werewolf costumes are made at the Haunted Verdun Manor. Lots of pictures demonstrate the process.

 Werewolves

INDEX